Patterns in the park

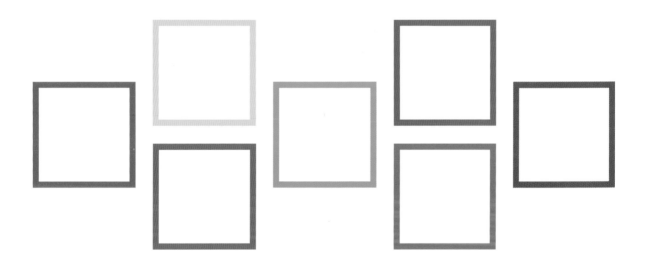

Lisa Bruce

Heinemann
LIBRARY

Little Nippers

www.heinemann.co.uk/library
Visit our website to find out more information about **Heinemann Library** books.

To order:
☎ Phone 44 (0) 1865 888066
▤ Send a fax to 44 (0) 1865 314091
▥ Visit the Heinemann Bookshop at www.heinemann.co.uk/library to browse our catalogue and order online.

First published in Great Britain by Heinemann Library, Halley Court, Jordan Hill, Oxford OX2 8EJ, part of Harcourt Education. Heinemann is a registered trademark of Harcourt Education Ltd.

Editorial: Jilly Attwood and Claire Throp
Design: Jo Hinton-Malivoire and bigtop, Bicester, UK
Models made by: Jo Brooker
Picture Research: Rosie Garai
Production: Séverine Ribierre

Originated by Dot Gradations
Printed and bound in China by South China Printing Company

ISBN 0 431 17193 9 (hardback)
07 06 05 04 03
10 9 8 7 6 5 4 3 2 1

ISBN 0 431 17198 X (paperback)
07 06 05 04 03
10 9 8 7 6 5 4 3 2 1

British Library Cataloguing in Publication Data
Bruce, Lisa
Patterns in the park – (Maths all around us)
516.1'5
A full catalogue record for this book is available from the British Library.

Acknowledgements
The Publishers would like to thank the following for permission to reproduce photographs: Ace Stock p. **18–19**; Alamy pp. **7**, **15**; Garden Picture Library p. **21** (Alec Scaresbrook); Gareth Boden p. **20**; Getty Images p. **8**, p. **16** (Nick Dolding); ImageState p. **9**; KPT Power Photos p. **17**; Trevor Clifford pp. **4**, **8**, **10**, **11**, **12**, **13**, **22–23**.

Cover photograph reproduced with permission of Masterfile/Peter Griffith.

The publishers would like to thank Annie Davy for her assistance in the preparation of this book.

Every effort has been made to contact copyright holders of any material reproduced in this book. Any omissions will be rectified in subsequent printings if notice is given to the publishers.

Contents

Patterns

The park is full of patterns.

Circles

Some patterns are made from circles.

Spotty

Dotty

Curves

If you throw a pebble in the pond it makes a pattern of circles, which get **bigger** and **bigger.**

spiral

The snail's shell
has a curly pattern
called a spiral.

Squares

Some patterns
are made
from squares.

Rectangles

Some patterns are made with rectangles, like the bricks in this wall.

Or the wood in this fence.

Stripes

Stripes are straight patterns using different colours.

What can you see that has stripes?

15

Colours

The pattern on this kite is made from two different colours.

There are also two different colours on this football.

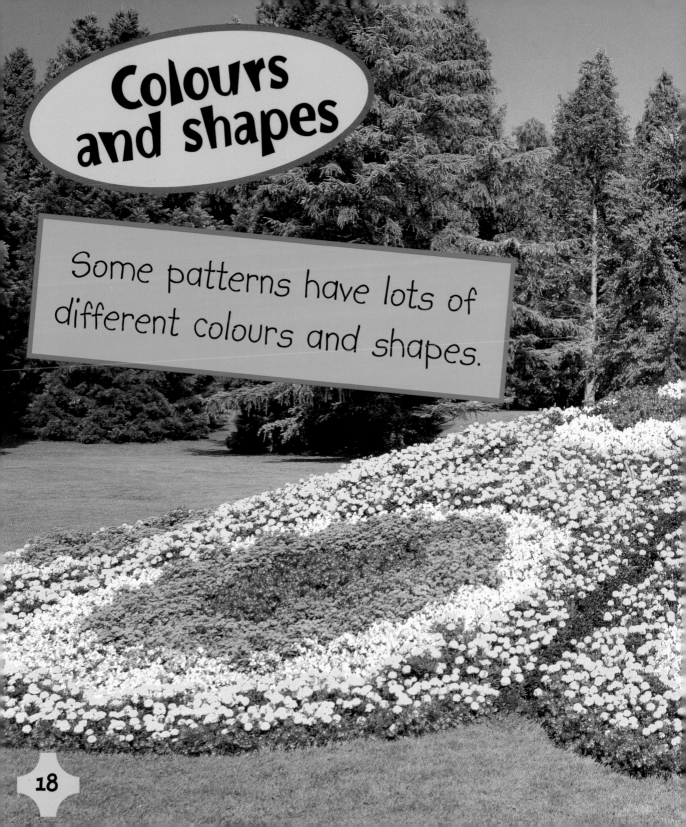

Colours and shapes

Some patterns have lots of different colours and shapes.

Making patterns

Some people make patterns from things they find in the park.

pine cones

twigs

What could you use to
make a pattern?

leaves

stones

Six children playing in the sun.
They should all wear hats.
You choose the right one.

Can you say which hat the last boy should put on to complete the pattern?

Index

The end

Notes for adults

Maths all around us introduces children to basic mathematical concepts. The four books will help to form the foundation for later work in science and mathematics. The following Early Learning Goals are relevant to this series:
• say and use number names in order in familiar contexts
• count reliably up to 10 everyday objects
• recognise numerals 1 to 9
• use language, such as 'more' or 'less' to compare two numbers
• talk about, recognise and recreate simple patterns
• use language, such as 'circle' or 'bigger', to describe the shape and size of solids and flat shapes.

The *Maths all around us* series explores shapes, counting, patterns and sizes using familiar environments and objects to show children that there is maths all around us. The series will encourage children to think more about the structure of different objects around them, and the relationships between them. It will also provide opportunities for discussing the importance of maths in a child's daily life. This series will encourage children to experience how different shapes feel, and to see how patterns can be made with shapes.

Patterns in the park will help children extend their vocabulary, as they will hear new words such as *patterns*, *circles*, *spiral*, *curly*, *squares*, *rectangles*, *stripes*, *different* and *complete*.

Follow-up activities
• Let a tap drip into a bowl of water and ask what pattern the water forms (i.e. circles).
• Using two different colours of paint, ask one child to create a pattern on a sheet of paper. See if others can copy it.
• Collect items from the park or garden and use them to make patterns.